SCHAFFHSN.

BODEN-SEE

THURGAU

RH.FALL
STEIN

ROMANS-HORN
ARBON

IRCHEL
THUR
FRAUENFELD

ADEN
ZÜRICH
WINTERTHUR
TOSS

SITTE
ST.GALLEN

LIMMAT
ZÜRICH
GREIFEN-SEE
PFÄFFIKON
ZÜRICH-SEE

ST.

HERISAU
ALT-
STÄTTEN
APPENZELL

GALLEN

ZUG
RAPPERSWIL
SÄNTIS
2504
WILDHAUS

ZUG
AEGERI-SEE
EINSIEDELN

THUR
WERDENBG.
WALEN-STADT
WALENSEE

SNACHT
RIGI
1800
SCHWYZ
SCHWYZ

LINTH
GLARUS
GLÄRNISCH
2920
BRAUNWALD

LIECH-TEN-STEIN

STANS
RÜTLI

GLARUS

SARGAN

URI
2932
ROTSTOCK
FLÜELEN
ALTDORF

BAD RAGAZ

PRÄTIGAU

ENGELBERG
KLAUSENPASS

RHEIN

KLOSTERS

SCHULS

SUSTEN-PASS
URI

VORDERRHEIN

CHUR

DORF
DAVOS
PLATZ
AROSA

SUSCH
INN
ENGADIN

GÖSCHENEN
SCHÖLLENEN
OBERALP-PASS

FLÜELA-PASS
UNTER-
ZERNEZ
TARASP

ANDERMATT
LUKMANIER-PASS

TIEFENKASTEL

OBERENGADIN

NATIONALPARK

LTSCH
TUNNEL
AIROLO
GOTTHARD
FURKA PASS

THUSIS
VIA MALA

GRAU BÜNDEN
ALBULA PASS

INN

OFEN-PASS

HINTERRHEIN
SPLÜGEN

UMBRAIL PASS

SAN BERNARDINO
SPLÜGEN-PASS

ST.MORITZ
JULIER-PASS
PONTRESINA

TICINO

SILS
BERNINA-PASS

MAGGIA

TICINO

MALOJAPASS

V.SCHÄFER
56

LOCARNO
TICINO

BELLINZONA
MONTE CENERI

N

LUGANO

LAGO MAGGIORE

LAGO DI LUGANO

KM   10   20   30   40   50

Switzerland

Switzerland

by OTTO SIEGNER

OFFICE DU LIVRE · FRIBOURG / SWITZERLAND

Preface
by Jacques Heffe

If school children of any country were given the task of drawing a Swiss landscape, what would most likely be the constant features? There would be a lake, a chalet amid lush alpine meadows with grazing cows and, overshadowing all, a mountain chain covered with perennial snow. However naive such drawings might appear, they would nevertheless be essentially true. Switzerland mainly impresses the stranger with her manifold scenic attractions; her very name conjures up the image of snowy mountain peaks, precipices and raging torrents and of meadows, woods and clear lakes, instead of cathedrals, palaces and museums, as would be the case with France or Italy. Nature endowed this small country with all these charms, determined her natural boundaries, and so, to a large degree, predetermined her history. In the course of the great revolution which, in Western Europe, succeeded the Renaissance and Classicism, there developed a longing for nature and, naturally, people began looking towards Switzerland, the sparkling jewel in the heart of Europe. Hardly any other country can boast of so much enthusiastic praise by the poets; Rousseau, Goethe, Albrecht von Haller, Lord Byron, Victor Hugo — to name a few — expressed so strong an admiration for this tiny country that an ever-growing stream of tourists from all parts of the globe began to follow their example. Thus Switzerland became the classical tourists' and vacation resort, the "playground of Europe", which she will remain as long as there are people looking for rest, relaxation and new pleasure in life, amid magnificent landscapes. Switzerland is a small country which, even at its widest, may be crossed within a few hours by train or car; and yet it appears quite large to the traveller. First, because the variety of impressions cannot be compressed into such a small frame and also because there are no straight roads in the country, and one arrives at one's destination only by various detours which, by constantly changing direction, first to the right and then to the left and, above all, by ups and downs, pleasantly prolong the trip. All of a sudden, the scene will change and, in rapid succession, the traveller finds himself reis a democrat by birth. He has never recognized any other but his own sovereignty, and his distrust of anyone gaining too much personal power has made him prefer the corporate form of government. We still find the last instance of pure democracy, in the cantons of Appenzell, Glarus and Unterwalden, where the voters assemble for the "Landsgemeinde" where they elect their representatives by raising their hands, decide about proposed laws and give their opinion in regard to taxes as well as to other public matters. Such democratic institutions have made it possible that people of different habits, languages and creeds live together in complete harmony. The stranger will enjoy an atmosphere of tranquillity, order and respect for the individual, his pleasure enhanced even by the fact that here he will find a country where − up to a point − the style of living could still be maintained to which the rest of Europe was accustomed before the war of 1939 or even that of 1914. Let us consider that Switzerland − except for the brief Napoleonic Occupation − has enjoyed peace since the 16th century, having been spared the horrors of two cruel wars which completely changed the European scene. But the Swiss could carry on their accustomed lives, keep their ideals and let things develop naturally without a cleft between the past and the present. So Switzerland has remained one of the few countries where a stranger may joyously breathe an atmosphere which, in many cases, he has never known but still unconsciously missed in his own country.

We have attempted to describe how Switzerland holds in readiness ever-new attractions which fascinate the stranger, and if we mainly dwelt upon the varied and beautiful landscapes, the incomparable institutions and the pervasive spirit of peace and order, the reader might easily reach the conclusion that this is merely a pastoral country whose towns could be neither numerous nor very interesting. But this is quite wrong, for even if there is no metropolis, no centre of the whole commercial, cultural and social life, setting the pace for the whole country, there is no provincial town either, which could be overshadowed by it. Every large Swiss town is a

capital of a sovereign state with its own history and traditions, and so they could all preserve their own native character. Even the most fashionable towns visibly express their close relationship with the past. If, late at night, one walks through the arcaded streets of Berne with their colourfully painted fountains and then stops for a moment at the Gerechtigkeitsgasse or Junkerngasse near the Minster, one can feel oneself transported back to the 16th or 17th century. There is also a picturesque old quarter in Geneva which is of unique character. We find the real city, Calvin's home, in the narrow, angular lanes, the quiet squares and the beautiful, severe façades in the vicinity of the St. Pierre Cathedral, the Bourg de Four and the Rue de la Cité.

Many Swiss cities have a marvellous location, on a lake, as Lucerne, Lausanne, Zurich, Lugano, or Geneva, or they nestle in a river-bend, as Berne, Fribourg or Basle. We are tempted to believe that the founders were troubled by no other worry than that of finding the most beautiful site. There is hardly a town from which one cannot catch a glimpse of a lake, a wood, a hill or snowy mountain. Perhaps it is this proximity to nature which lends such a healthy appearance to all the towns. During the summer this impression is enhanced even by the glorious blaze of flowers which abound in streets and squares, spreading an atmosphere of festive gaiety; so it is almost a wonder that the geranium has not already usurped the position of the edelweiss as the symbol of the Swiss flora. This also explains why a growing number of tourists make a stay in the towns a part of their holidays. There, one will discover that Switzerland also possesses considerable treasures of art such as one hardly imagined. Switzerland has much that remains from all the different cultural epochs which ever touched the country, especially from the Roman and the Early Christian period. Political stability and long periods of peace have always been beneficial to art and the preservation of its treasures. We must point out here that the political and social development of the country have played a more important part in this than may be commonly imagined.

There were no wealthy patrons of the arts such as the great princely houses and the ruling power; here the canton naturally could not compete with the pomp and splendour of the great European courts. Most of the architectural monuments of the cities therefore served some practical public purpose, for instance, as churches, town halls, granaries, and arsenals, and all of these buildings are consequently adapted to their surroundings and do not affect the general impression of simple harmony. In all these cases we find that the manner of artistic expression agrees with the demands of daily life. At Berne, Basle, Fribourg and Lausanne, we find some beautiful town halls in Late Gothic, but this does not mean that only these large towns have notable buildings. Even the small towns like Sursee, Appenzell or Le Landeron can boast of charming architectural works. To a larger extent even than the town halls, the churches served as meeting-places for the people. The towns took great pride in building lovely churches, adorning them for the honour of God and of their own town also. The Baptistry of Riva San Vitale in the Ticino, from around the year 500, is perhaps the oldest intact Christian monument of Switzerland. There are countless Romanesque remains, as the Lombardic churches of the Ticino. To name only a few of the best-known, there are: the Church of St. Sulpice, that of St. Pierre de Clages in the Valais, the Benedictine Abbey of Payerne, All Saints' Convent at Schaffhausen and the Great Cathedral at Zurich. From the Gothic period might be mentioned: the Cathedral of Lausanne, a perfect example of Early Gothic, the Cathedrals of Geneva and of Fribourg, the Collegiate Church of Neuchâtel, the Minster of Basle, especially remarkable for its magnificent sculptures. Even though Baroque, in contrast to other styles, touched Switzerland less, the few — mostly ecclesiastical — structures of this period are yet of considerable importance, as for instance, the Convent Church of Einsiedeln, or the Collegiate Church of St. Gallen.

Limited space prohibits more than a few brief hints in regard to Swiss architecture. But we must not omit all mention of the numerous mountain churches and chapels which — with touching simplicity — merge in their marvellous surroundings. Above all in the Grisons and the Valais, we find many such places of prayer and meditation as, for instance, the delightful little church of Fex above Sils in the Engadine, standing white and tiny, amidst mighty peaks. Throughout the country there are churches and castles of impressive aspect — we need scarcely mention the famous Chillon Castle on Lake Geneva — all of which fit into their surroundings most agreeably. To look at the exterior of these structures only would be a pity, as the interior often reveals the real treasures. The museums are also well worth seeing, such as the State Museum at Zurich and the historical museums at Berne, Basle or Geneva which have collections of priceless value. Native art, always flourishing and greatly fostered in Switzerland, has produced many noteworthy works which — though not of paramount importance — still reveal much of the spirit and the make-up of a section of the nation. The unique features of the landscape could never be better expressed than in these works of native art, just as the human traits are best exhibited in the local festivals, some of which have been upheld to this day. In this connection we ought to mention the vintners' festivals, the alpine festivals, Shrove Tuesday carnival at Basle, the "Sechseläuten" at Zurich and the "Schlittedas" of the Engadine.

Apart from the attractions which Switzerland possesses in its scenery, its people and its art treasures, there is the added attraction that all these treasures are so easily and pleasurably accessible. Looking after the tourists has here been developed to a perfection rarely found anywhere else. No effort for the benefit of the tourist's comfort is spared, a fact to which Switzerland's high international reputation owes much. As vacationers are often atracted to the remoter mountain regions, no effort has been spared to offer those who are unused to the hardships of mountaineering every opportunity of gaining experience of the whole beauty of the alpine world. Alpine railroads, funiculars, suspension railways and ski-lifts open up a tual liberality, to the Swiss cultural centres. Its University and College of Advanced Technology enjoy international fame; events of artistic and cultural note follow one after another throughout the year. The museums deserve special mention: The National Museum near the Station is a collection displaying the Swiss cultural heritage of many centuries. In order to make it a really national institution, no entrance fee is charged. Probably without peer in the whole world is the Rietberg Collection: ancient Oriental and non-European works of art of transcendent craftmanship, which, in their essential simplicity frequently have quite a modern air. The corridors of the City Hall, too, are one continuous art gallery: here, contemporary Swiss painters and sculptors have a possibility of providing an artistic pleasure for the Zurich citizens on business in the City Hall, in passing – so to speak. Looked at in this way, the designation given to Zurich, even as a trading centre, the "Athens on the Limmat" is completely justified.

The Cantons of Grisons and Glarus

Pages 66 — 107

Grisons, the largest but most sparsely populated canton, is a world of its own. It is called the land of the 150 valleys but one ought to count the mountains really! Furrowed, divided and walled-in, this is a land of a thousand aspects in a country which itself is not remarkable for its simplicity. Even the languages reveals this multiplicity, for they are a Swiss-German dialect, Italian and Rhaeto-Romanic, the fourth official language which is still in use in the Valley of the Vorderrhein (Near Rhine) and in the Inn Valley. Grisons is noteworthy also for its superb mountain landscapes and the picturesque villages with typical, indigenous houses.

The capital, Chur (from the Roman Curia), is a friendly town where the houses – decorated with wrought iron-work – extend from the shore of the Rhine up to the Bishop's Palace. The Rhine is still young and wild there but already vineyards, yielding a pleasant, light wine, spread out from its banks. As the other places do not exceed the size of large market villages, Chur is the only proper town in all Grisons. These places, amid an enchanting landscape, are mostly holiday and winter-sports resorts and every one of them has a particular attraction of its own. So Flims has its larch woods; Davos, a wide, sunny valley at the foot of magnificent mountains and St. Moritz, a crystal-clear lake, all of which enhances the charm of the country. Others are Arosa, Lenzerheide, Pontresina, Schuls-Tarasp, but we are well aware that we have had to neglect quite a few equally attractive places. It is a dilemma to have to decide whether to spend the summer there, or the winter, which spreads the slopes with a carpet of snow, changing the countryside into a skiing-ground. Despite the ever increasing tourism, Grisons has retained its original character. There are numerous palatial hotels in the valley of the Engadine which, particularly in the upper region with its tranquil, silvery lakes, seems bathed in the light and purity of a new world. Between Zernez and the Minster Valley extends the National Park; it is of singular beauty. A view into the wild Chuozza Valley alone or the panorama from the 7,070 ft. Ofen Pass in the Ortler Group would justify a lengthy trip, and the Umbrail Pass, the highest road-pass of Switzerland (8,219 ft.) and a trip over the Stilfserjoch (9,094 ft.) leave striking impressions. The Italian part of the canton is represented by the three valleys of Pushglav, Bergell and Misox (Val Mesocco). Whether one visits the lonely villages at the foot of Mt. Silvretta, mounts the Julier, Bernina or St. Bernardino Passes, or rides along the Via Mala, once an awe-inspiring road through the gorge of the Rhine Valley, or goes to Davos for skiing or Arosa as a convalescent, whether one seeks quiet lakes and silent larch woods, or looks for the pulsating life of fashionable international resorts, one will be surprised to find all this in Grisons, enhanced even through its perfect harmony;

There were no wealthy patrons of the arts such as the great princely houses and the ruling power; here the canton naturally could not compete with the pomp and splendour of the great European courts. Most of the architectural monuments of the cities therefore served some practical public purpose, for instance, as churches, town halls, granaries, and arsenals, and all of these buildings are consequently adapted to their surroundings and do not affect the general impression of simple harmony. In all these cases we find that the manner of artistic expression agrees with the demands of daily life. At Berne, Basle, Fribourg and Lausanne, we find some beautiful town halls in Late Gothic, but this does not mean that only these large towns have notable buildings. Even the small towns like Sursee, Appenzell or Le Landeron can boast of charming architectural works. To a larger extent even than the town halls, the churches served as meeting-places for the people. The towns took great pride in building lovely churches, adorning them for the honour of God and of their own town also. The Baptistry of Riva San Vitale in the Ticino, from around the year 500, is perhaps the oldest intact Christian monument of Switzerland. There are countless Romanesque remains, as the Lombardic churches of the Ticino. To name only a few of the best-known, there are: the Church of St. Sulpice, that of St. Pierre de Clages in the Valais, the Benedictine Abbey of Payerne, All Saints' Convent at Schaffhausen and the Great Cathedral at Zurich. From the Gothic period might be mentioned: the Cathedral of Lausanne, a perfect example of Early Gothic, the Cathedrals of Geneva and of Fribourg, the Collegiate Church of Neuchâtel, the Minster of Basle, especially remarkable for its magnificent sculptures. Even though Baroque, in contrast to other styles, touched Switzerland less, the few — mostly ecclesiastical — structures of this period are yet of considerable importance, as for instance, the Convent Church of Einsiedeln, or the Collegiate Church of St. Gallen.

Limited space prohibits more than a few brief hints in regard to Swiss architecture. But we must not omit all mention of the numerous mountain churches and chapels which — with touching simplicity — merge in their marvellous surroundings. Above all in the Grisons and the Valais, we find many such places of prayer and meditation as, for instance, the delightful little church of Fex above Sils in the Engadine, standing white and tiny, amidst mighty peaks. Throughout the country there are churches and castles of impressive aspect — we need scarcely mention the famous Chillon Castle on Lake Geneva — all of which fit into their surroundings most agreeably. To look at the exterior of these structures only would be a pity, as the interior often reveals the real treasures. The museums are also well worth seeing, such as the State Museum at Zurich and the historical museums at Berne, Basle or Geneva which have collections of priceless value. Native art, always flourishing and greatly fostered in Switzerland, has produced many noteworthy works which — though not of paramount importance — still reveal much of the spirit and the make-up of a section of the nation. The unique features of the landscape could never be better expressed than in these works of native art, just as the human traits are best exhibited in the local festivals, some of which have been upheld to this day. In this connection we ought to mention the vintners' festivals, the alpine festivals, Shrove Tuesday carnival at Basle, the "Sechseläuten" at Zurich and the "Schlittedas" of the Engadine.

Apart from the attractions which Switzerland possesses in its scenery, its people and its art treasures, there is the added attraction that all these treasures are so easily and pleasurably accessible. Looking after the tourists has here been developed to a perfection rarely found anywhere else. No effort for the benefit of the tourist's comfort is spared, a fact to which Switzerland's high international reputation owes much. As vacationers are often atracted to the remoter mountain regions, no effort has been spared to offer those who are unused to the hardships of mountaineering every opportunity of gaining experience of the whole beauty of the alpine world. Alpine railroads, funiculars, suspension railways and ski-lifts open up a

The Cantons of Basle, Aargau, Schaffhausen, Thurgau, St. Gallen, Appenzell and Zurich

Pages 21 – 65

The northern cantons of Switzerland as named above, stretch from Basle, the "Golden Gate of Switzerland", up the Rhine to the Lake of Constance. With its little towns of mediaeval appearance, with romantic castles and strongholds and the gently rolling country-side, this part of Switzerland does not correspond at all to the Switzerland which the foreigner pictures to himself. Basle, having more than 200,000 inhabitants, is one of the most important Swiss towns, also one with the greatest wealth of tradition. Trade has played a decisive role for centuries; industry has also established a centre here which sends out high-grade products all over the world and finally, this cathedral city on the sharp bend of the Rhine has been the enduring home of intellectual and cultural life in Switzerland for centuries. In 1460, Pope Pius II founded the University which, in the days of Erasmus of Rotterdam, was the centre of humanism and which has been able to maintain its considerable reputation down to our times. Noble, secular buildings, among them the City Hall, evidence the wealth of its citizens; the Gallus Gate with its sculptures testifies to their feeling for art.

Aarau, the cantonal capital of the Aargau, unites the charm of a picturesque town with the animation of a modern, industrial centre. The same applies to Baden, the seat of the Brown-Boveri Works; this ancient thermal spa was visited by the Romans. Quite close by, lies the 13th century Abbey of Wettingen, famous for the Gothic church with its richly carved choirstalls and noteworthy stained-glass windows.

Travelling up the Rhine from Basle, via the saline spa of Rheinfelden, Laufenburg and Coblenz (at the confluence of the Aare with the Rhine), one arrives at Schaffhausen. This small cantonal capital embedded in vineyards is well-known, unjustly, mainly for "its" waterfall. The waters of Europe's greatest fall plunge, actually, near Neuhausen, almost two miles away. The falls are almost 200 feet wide. Stein on Rhine, with its frescoed houses, with their gables and oriels, the Roman bridge and the stronghold over the river, the fine Town Hall, the mediaeval marketplace or the Witches' Tower produces the same effect as a town in a picture book.

Leaving the Lake, we approach St. Gallen, the centre for Swiss embroideries and choice textiles. The Irish monk, Gallus, founded an abbey here in the 7th century. The Abbey church (baroque) and the library with its costly manuscripts are ranked among the most important records of Swiss culture. Up the Rhine Valley, one comes upon Sargans with its proud fortress. Westward lies the Lake of Walen with its deep-green water and villages clinging to the precipitous cliffs. South of St. Gallen lies the Canton of Appenzell, one of the most genuinely original Swiss ones. The population, mostly dairy farmers, loyally and strictly preserve their old customs and habits. The market-town of Appenzell delights the visitor with its Late-Gothic Town Hall, the lovely fountains and its sparklingly clean houses. Returning from the countrified Appenzell to Zurich, one can imagine one has been transposed to another world. Zurich is not only the largest, but also the busiest, most industrialised and wealthiest of all Swiss towns — one with pronounced city-characteristics, which is not to say that its charm has diminished at all. This aspect of the city is maintained by the old guild-halls on the Limmat Quay, the churches, whose bells are tuned to chime harmoniously, the picturesque alleys of the old quarter and the enchanting surroundings. On the shore of Lake Zurich, sheltered in the midst of gentle, wooded slopes, it seems to be in a vast garden where one can enjoy a magnificent view of the Glarus Alps. The slogan used by the local tourist office hits the nail on the head with its "Lake-side Garden-City". Even though Zurich is, above all, a business and trading centre, it belongs, nevertheless, on account of its intellectual liberality, to the Swiss cultural centres. Its University and College of Advanced Technology enjoy international fame; events of artistic and cultural note follow one after another throughout the year. The museums deserve special mention: The National Museum near the Station is a collection displaying the Swiss cultural heritage of many centuries. In order to make it a really national institution, no entrance fee is charged. Probably without peer in the whole world is the Rietberg Collection: ancient Oriental and non-European works of art of transcendent craftmanship, which, in their essential simplicity frequently have quite a modern air. The corridors of the City Hall, too, are one continuous art gallery: here, contemporary Swiss painters and sculptors have a possibility of providing an artistic pleasure for the Zurich citizens on business in the City Hall, in passing — so to speak. Looked at in this way, the designation given to Zurich, even as a trading centre, the "Athens on the Limmat" is completely justified.

The Cantons of Grisons and Glarus

Pages 66 — 107

Grisons, the largest but most sparsely populated canton, is a world of its own. It is called the land of the 150 valleys but one ought to count the mountains really! Furrowed, divided and walled-in, this is a land of a thousand aspects in a country which itself is not remarkable for its simplicity. Even the languages reveals this multiplicity, for they are a Swiss-German dialect, Italian and Rhaeto-Romanic, the fourth official language which is still in use in the Valley of the Vorderrhein (Near Rhine) and in the Inn Valley. Grisons is noteworthy also for its superb mountain landscapes and the picturesque villages with typical, indigenous houses.

The capital, Chur (from the Roman Curia), is a friendly town where the houses — decorated with wrought iron-work — extend from the shore of the Rhine up to the Bishop's Palace. The Rhine is still young and wild there but already vineyards, yielding a pleasant, light wine, spread out from its banks. As the other places do not exceed the size of large market villages, Chur is the only proper town in all Grisons. These places, amid an enchanting landscape, are mostly holiday and winter-sports resorts and every one of them has a particular attraction of its own. So Flims has its larch woods; Davos, a wide, sunny valley at the foot of magnificent mountains and St. Moritz, a crystal-clear lake, all of which enhances the charm of the country. Others are Arosa, Lenzerheide, Pontresina, Schuls-Tarasp, but we are well aware that we have had to neglect quite a few equally attractive places. It is a dilemma to have to decide whether to spend the summer there, or the winter, which spreads the slopes with a carpet of snow, changing the country-side into a skiing-ground. Despite the ever increasing tourism, Grisons has retained its original character. There are numerous palatial hotels in the valley of the Engadine which, particularly in the upper region with its tranquil, silvery lakes, seems bathed in the light and purity of a new world. Between Zernez and the Minster Valley extends the National Park; it is of singular beauty. A view into the wild Chuozza Valley alone or the panorama from the 7,070 ft. Ofen Pass in the Ortler Group would justify a lengthy trip, and the Umbrail Pass, the highest road-pass of Switzerland (8,219 ft.) and a trip over the Stilfserjoch (9,094 ft.) leave striking impressions. The Italian part of the canton is represented by the three valleys of Pushglav, Bergell and Misox (Val Mesocco). Whether one visits the lonely villages at the foot of Mt. Silvretta, mounts the Julier, Bernina or St. Bernardino Passes, or rides along the Via Mala, once an awe-inspiring road through the gorge of the Rhine Valley, or goes to Davos for skiing or Arosa as a convalescent, whether one seeks quiet lakes and silent larch woods, or looks for the pulsating life of fashionable international resorts, one will be surprised to find all this in Grisons, enhanced even through its perfect harmony;

this Canton is justly called a miniature Switzerland in it-self. Only a little farther to the west we reach the shore of the Lake of Wallenstadt, probably the most romantic of all Swiss lakes; its dark-green water reminds one of the lakes of the fairy tales. A few villages only edge the shores, which soon rise to the steep heights of the mighty, cleft mountain massif of the Churfirsten, which gives the land-scape a striking calm and, at the same time, an awe-inspiring aspect.

After crossing the Kerenz, the small pass with a view almost all the way across Lake Wallenstadt, one reaches Linthtal, whose steep sides cut deep into the mountains opening towards Zurich. Encircling mountains mark this Canton of Glarus, which is partly pastoral and partly industrial. The steep cliff-faces dominating the valley are broken only by a few terraces with several villages. Braun-wald is the best known of them, a summer and winter resort which may be reached from the valley by means of the funicular. Glarus, the cantonese capital, is a peaceful little town. The greatest yearly event there is the "Lands-gemeinde", a convention of all cantonese citizens who assemble to decide public matters. Several side-valleys branch off from the Linthtal, the most picturesque being the Klöntal with its pastures, woods and small trout lake. Across the Klausen Pass, leading to Altdorf near Lake Lucerne, this shut-in canton has access to the St. Gotthard region and central Switzerland.

The Cantons of Berne, Uri, Schwyz, Unterwalden, Lucerne, Zug and Solothurn

Pages 108 – 163

Berne is the Swiss capital and so the seat of its Federal Assembly, the Government and the diplomatic represent-atives of foreign states — but above all, however, the cantonal capital.

Agriculture is the determinant factor in the Canton of Berne; this is demonstrated even in the city; in its countri-fied air of snugness; its narrow, twisting alleys, comfortable inns and old fountains. For the collector of antiques and furniture of sterling quality, Berne is a veritable paradise. The wealth of offers in the antique shops standing cheek by jowl make one confused, although it must be said that the prices are all within an acceptable range. Preserved from its glorious past, Berne has also an aspect of dignified strength, however, which appears, above all, in its spacious streets in the city's centre with mighty arcades like covered parapet walks, the ancient city-gates and the centuries-old façades of the houses. Where, in Europe, is there another city which has preserved its mediæval air so well? Berne — the name is derived from "bears". Consequently, in the old moat the city keeps living heraldic beasts, which per-form amusing antics at the bottom of the pit in return for the food the children give them. The entire Bernese country imparts an impression of reliability, comfort and luxuriant growth, as does the capital. The large farm-houses breathe of prosperity as well as the little towns, where past and present harmonize pleasantly. Thun, Spiez — neat and shining holiday-resorts to please one, on the way to the Oberland — are, year after year, the popular tourist centres for recreation on the Lake of Thun. Inter-laken, lying between two sharply contrasting lakes, is a more fashionable holiday-resort and the point of departure for trips into the Bernese Oberland. Those who wish to keep their distance from the mighty massifs remain here; those who wish to penetrate into the heart of the Oberland, how-ever, make excursions from here, to the health-resorts of Grindelwald, Wengen, Mürren or Lauterbrunnen — all easily accessible by excellent railways. In this district, the nature-loving walker finds an abundance of mountain tours of all degrees of difficulty awaiting him, from the easy ascent to the peaks (by the Jungfrau Railway) to the riskiest alpine climbs or glacier and ski tours, which can scarcely be excell-ed anywhere. Not far from Brienz, one finds alpine roads of renown, which lead over the passes of Grimsel, Susten or Brünig into the Valais, the Canton of Uri or to Lucerne.

The district round Lake Lucerne is not only the heart of Switzerland geographically but also historically, for here the State was born, more than 650 years ago. Lucerne itself is not only an important tourist centre on the Lake itself and one with very attractive mountain view-points as Rigi, Pilatus and Bürgenstock, it is, in addition, historically interesting. In the old Confederacy it played a great part. Still preserved from this period are treasured monuments – the Gothic Town Hall on the Corn Market, from 1602; the Palace Chapel (built 735 and restored after a fire in 1639) which has two slender spires. Nor must one omit the old, covered, wooden bridge over the Reuss, with its paintings; the seven towers of the ramparts; old churches and the narrow streets in which two cars cannot pass. Lucerne is a town with particularly good hotels. How could it be otherwise?

Above the shores of the Lake of Urn – the name given to the most outlying arm of the Lake of Lucerne, a road has been hewn out of the mountain side, which leads to the Urn country, the home of the Swiss national hero, William Tell. Here is not the place to question what is truth in the history of this man. In his drama "Wilhelm Tell", Schiller gave this man such prominence that, today, he has become an "institution". Many great alpine roads start at Altdorf, Uri's cantonal capital; one, the Klausen Pass Road leads to the Glarus country; the one going over the Susten Pass, built some twenty years ago, leads to the Bernese Oberland, the Oberalp Road leads into the Vorder Rhine Valley and further, over the St. Gotthard after a memorable passage through a wild, stratified gorge into Ticino and on to the South. Schwyz and Unterwalden, lying on either side of the Lake of Lucerne, are, like Uri, engaged in agriculture, dairy-farming and field tillage as well as forestry, present, however, a somewhat less wild landscape.

Lakes and mountains, lush meadows and trim parks, the most excellently constructed roads and well-cared-for paths for walkers make this district practically the hub of the Swiss tourist traffic. Several hundred years ago, though, "Old Original Switzerland", as this region round

Lake Lucerne is called, was the heart of the little republic. Around this district, in the course of a centuries of its history, the other cantons have gathered to coalesce finally into the "Confoederatio Helvetica".

The Cantons of Geneva, Fribourg, Neuchâtel, Vaud and Valais
Pages 164 – 225

The French-speaking district of Switzerland includes all three elements determining the geographical structure of the whole land: Jura Mountains, the Central Plains and the Alps. Let's begin our short but interesting journey with the region round the Lake of Geneva, where, on the surrounding slopes, extensive vineyards spread out – the cradle of much-appreciated wines. Behind, the Savoy Alps are glimpsed. On the shores of the Lakes of Neuchâtel, Bienne (Biel) and Morat, the climate is pleasant and mild. The lakes of the Jura, the Lac de Joux or the Lac des Brenets with their pine woods remind one rather of the lakes of Scandinavia.

Valais, a region somewhat on the flank of the rest of Switzerland and ringed round by its high mountains, comprises the valley of the Rhône from its source to its entry into the Lake of Geneva. The wide, sunny Rhône lowlands are one continuous garden, where excellent vines as well as fruit grow. The charming picture changes, however, as soon as one penetrates into one of the numerous lateral valleys leading up to the High Alps. Here, the alpinist finds a choice of mountain tours which can scarcely be excelled anywhere; from such well-known holiday centres as Zermatt or Saas-Fee, he can climb the peaks of the Weißhorn, Matterhorn or Dufour. The little towns of the Rhône Valley, as the French-speaking cantonal capital of Sion, or Brig, where a Swiss-German dialect is spoken, jealously preserve their old characteristics. The love of inherited traditions shows itself even today, in the custom of wearing the regional costumes, especially in the lateral valleys such as Loetschental or Val d'Hérens. Where, in the old days, the travellers passing through Valais were priests, merchants and soldiers, today it is holiday-makers who troop along the well-built roads of the canton. At the southwest corner of the Lake of Geneva, just where the Rhône flows out, lies Geneva with its landmarks, visible from afar; the Cathedral of St. Pierre, which dominates the old city, Calvin's home, and the fountain, "Jet d'eau", some 394 feet high, symbolizing the second rôle of Geneva, that of a recreation centre for holiday-makers and tourists. We must not forget though that there is a third aspect of Geneva, the city of international institutions and the Red Cross.

Lausanne, spreading out over its sunny hillsides, which slope down to its harbour at Ouchy, is the City of Youth — and of steep streets. If one is surprised, at noon and in the evening, to meet so many young people near the venerable Church of St. Francis, the rendezvous of the whole town, the explanation is to be found in the fact that the University and innumerable other institutes attract pupils and students. And certainly, the reason why the streets of the town are so steep is that Lausanne people can slip down into Ouchy the more quickly in order to pass their leisure hours on the Promenade there.

Fribourg is the stronghold of Catholicism in Switzerland and is a bridge between the German-speaking region and the French-speaking region. Its entire old quarter, in a bend of the Soane, is a museum comprising old churches, bell-towers, monasteries and picturesque, old houses. On all sides stretch the wide, green pastures of the Fribourg country-side, where one discovers quaint little towns such as Bulle, Greyerz, Romont and Morat. This, last with its defensive walls, the covered parapet walks, its ancient towers and gates and the main street with its arcaded houses must look just as it did at the time of the Battle of Murten where the army of Charles the Bold was beaten by the Confederates in 1476.

Neuchâtel, which is visible as a whole only from the water side, is distinctive owing to a warm golden glow which comes from the yellowish sandstone of which its houses are built. The distinguished appearance of the town stems, perhaps, from the old days when Neuchâtel had its dukes and was not a cantonal capital. Along the side of the lake with the same name are the little fishing villages and tiny towns engaged in wine-making, Auvernier, Concise and Grandson.

Further north in the Jura Mountains, at a height of 3281 feet, lies La Chaux-de-Fonds, the hub of Swiss watchmaking, whose importance is, at the most, only equalled by its neighbour, Le Locle. In contrast to most other Swiss towns, La Chaux-de-Fonds, with its symmetrical town-planning, is definitely modern. The Avenue Léopold-Robert, the main business street, the sky-scrapers and all the modern, practical facilities have a singular foil in the country-side of woods and pastures in the immediate vicinity of the town. How great the importance of the watchmaking industry is to the Swiss economy can be demonstrated by a single number: 40,000 Swiss earn a living working in this industry. A notable fact when the total population is 4.8 millions.

The Canton of Ticino

Pages 226—239

The Canton of Ticino is more distinctive than any other canton. It stretches farthest to the south; it possesses quite a different climate, namely one typical of Northern Italy; its official language is Italian and its inhabitants have characteristics which bring them closer to their neighbours to the south than they are to the people of Basle, Zurich or Geneva, for instance. Coming into Ticino from the north, especially on emerging from the Gotthard Tunnel, one could imagine that one had arrived suddenly in Italy. Here a sky of southern blue prevails, here the people speak

Italian as temperamentally and as passionately as further south. The farther one travels down the valley of the Leventina, the more luxuriant is the flora: cypresses, palms, fig-trees – more like a part of the Riviera. The little villages, their houses clustering round the church tower and clinging to the rock-face, could just as easily be situated some hundreds of kilometres southwards. The general impression is that Ticino is really a piece of Italy that has inadvertently slipped into Switzerland. With the Alps at ist back, it opens on to the wide Plain of Lombardy and its language and culture came from there. This obvious affinity with its great southern neighbour does not prevent the natives from being, with heart and soul, Swiss citizens, which has resulted from their common history going back to the 15th century. When the Ticino people had to decide on their future, they determined to be "Liberi e Svizzeri", i.e. free and Swiss and to join the Swiss Confederacy in 1803.

Ticino can be divided into three chief regions: the mountains, the valleys and the lakes. Let us begin with the last, as this region is the attraction and the goal of every trip to Ticino.

The long Lake Maggiore, into which the river flows which gives its name to the canton, belongs to Switzerland only at the northern end, where it bears the pleasant name of Verbano. Its shores are matchless, dotted with charming, small holiday-resorts. The largest is Locarno, whose pink and yellow houses, in the midst of palms, apricot and orange trees, and camellias, centre round a small bay. The neighbouring places, Ascona, Brissago, and Magadino – to name only a few – are, like Locarno, popular resorts. Beyond Mount Ceneri, the Lake of Lugano spreads its arms out between the mountains, whose slopes are planted with pines and chestnut trees. Here, embedded between Mount Bré and Mount Salvatore lies Lugano on its bay, which makes it resemble a miniature Rio de Janeiro. This marvellously situated town enjoys a mild climate; visitors are also attracted by its architecture of the most varied periods. The Ticino valleys are almost all wild and romantic. The way through the most important of them,

the Leventina, is barred in the south by the old capital and fortress, Bellinzona, within whose walls, three mighty, mediaeval castles and houses of a southern type of architecture are found in curious proximity.

The influence of the neighbour on the south—how could one expect otherwise – makes no halt before entering the kitchen. On the contrary, what is served in the little "grottos" as the pubs are called, not only bears an Italian name but consists mostly of original Italian dishes. Spaghetti served in all ways, risotto (rice) and excellent kinds of sausage: "mortaella", "salametti" and "cacciatori" (two kinds of salami), or a native dish made by the farmers themselves, "lughanighe nostrane". It stands to reason that the fresh vegetables grown in the "Garden of Switzerland" should be used to make the cantonal speciality, "minestrone". To add flavour to most of the dishes made, this region has an abundance of local kinds of cheese. A choice of over 30 various wines – Morcote, Brissago, Mezzane, or whatever name they bear – served in a little earthenware jug, a "boccalino", completes the enjoyment of every single meal.

*

In this land of so many waters, fish dishes are included in the "extra specials" – whether grilled, baked or boiled. The barbecued chickens are also well worth sampling, while the delicious fruit and the firm flesh of the Ticino hams should not be neglected. Having become accustomed to the Ticino ways of preparation, with olive oil, lots of onions, tomatoes and, above all, an abundance of little-known herbs – which one very quickly does – on returning home one feels there is some flavour missing. Consequently the Ticino cuisine is not the least among the attractions which draw so many visitors to the southernmost Swiss canton.

Index of pictures

Basel: das Spalentor, 1370 erbaut   Bâle: le «Spalentor»   Basle: The Spalen Gate   21

22   Basel, ein bedeutender
Umschlagplatz der Schweiz

Bâle: un important port de transit
en Suisse

Basle, an important Swiss entrepôt,
is linked …

Durch den Rhein ist Basel mit den Häfen
Hollands und der Nordsee verbunden

Le Rhin relie la ville aux ports
hollandais et à la mer du Nord

... by the Rhine to the harbours
of Holland and the North Sea

23

Basel: das Rathaus

Bâle: l'Hôtel de Ville

24   Basle's Town Hall

Traditionsreiches und prächtiges Fest Basels ist seine „Fasnacht" ▶

Le fameux «Carnaval» de Bâle, fête traditionnelle et merveilleuse

The most gorgeous and traditional festivities held in Basle are the "Fasnacht"

Augst bei Basel,
das um 27 v. Chr. von den Römern
gegründete „Augusta Raurica"
mit dem berühmten Amphitheater

Augst près de Bâle: fondée par les
Romains en 27 av. J.-C., sous le
nom de «Augusta Raurica», elle est
célèbre pour son amphithéâtre

Augst near Basle, with its famous
amphitheatre, is the "Augusta
Raurica" founded by the Romans
in 27 B. C.

Das altertümliche Laufenburg
am Rhein

Laufenbourg, petite cité médiévale
des bords du Rhin

Laufenburg,
on the Rhine, is ancient

27

Aarau, die Hauptstadt des Kantons
Aargau, am Südfuß des Jura

Aarau, la capitale du canton
d'Argovie

Aarau, the capital of the Canton
of Aargau

Aarburg mit der alten Burg
aus dem 11. Jahrhundert

Aarbourg et son vieux château
du XIᵉ siècle

Aarburg with the old fortress
dating from the 11th century

29

Olten: Blick auf die Altstadt
30   mit der Aare

Olten: la vieille ville que borde
le cours de l'Aar

Olten: view of the Old Town
with the Aar

Bremgarten, altes Städtchen an der Reuß mit Wehrtürmen und vielen anderen alten Bauten

Vieille cité construite sur la Reuss, Bremgarten possède encore d'anciennes tours fortifiées et autres constructions intéressantes

Bremgarten, an old town on the River Reuss, with defense towers and many other old buildings

31

Stein am Rhein, das wohlerhaltene
Städtchen aus dem Mittelalter
mit dem malerischen Marktplatz

L'Hôtel de Ville de Stein am Rhein
(XVIe siècle)
et la place du marché

The Town Hall (from the
16th century) and the picturesque
market square of Stein am Rhein

32

Blick auf das alte Städtchen
Lenzburg im Aargau

Vue sur Lenzburg, vieille cité
de l'Aargau

View of the little old town of
Lenzburg in the Aargau district

Baden an der Limmat,
war schon den Römern
als Schwefelbad bekannt

Baden, sur les bords de la Limmat,
ancienne station thermale déjà
connue des Romains

The sulphur-springs of Baden
on the Limmat were known even
to the Romans

36

Chorgestühl in der Klosterkirche
der ehemaligen Zisterzienser-Abtei
Wettingen, 1217 gegründet

Stalles de l'église de l'ancienne
abbaye cistercienne de Wettingen
qui avait été fondée en 1217

Choir-stalls in the church belonging
to the former Cistercian abbey of
Wettingen, founded 1217

Klosterkirche der Benediktiner-Abtei   L'église conventuelle de l'ancienne   Church of the Benedictine Abbey
Muri im Kanton Aargau   abbaye bénédictine de Muri   of Muri in Aargau   37

38   Zürich: Blick auf den Limmatquai   Zurich: vue sur le quai de la Limmat   View of Limmat Quay, Zurich

Blick auf die St. Peterskirche und
den Stadtkern von Zürich.
Im Vordergrund die Limmat

Vue sur l'église St-Pierre et le vieux
quartier du centre de Zurich.
Au premier plan, la Limmat

View of St. Peter's Church
and the city of Zurich on the
Limmat river

Das Rathaus von Zürich,
(1693 – 1698)
40   ein Spätrenaissancebau

L'Hôtel de Ville de Zurich,
une œuvre de la Renaissance
tardive (1693 – 1698)

The City Hall of Zurich,
built 1693 – 1698,
is in the late-renaissance style

Zürich: Das Großmünster und
das Zunfthaus „Zum Rüden"

Zurich: la cathédrale et la maison
«Zum Rüden»

The "Great Minster" of Zurich and
the Guildhall named "Zum Rüden"   41

Blick auf die Insel Ufenau und den
Damm von Rapperswil/Zürichsee

Vue sur l'île d'Ufenau et la digue
de Rapperswil dans le lac de Zurich

View of the Island of Ufenau and
the Rapperswil Dam on Lake Zurich

Rapperswil am Zürichsee. Hoch
über der Altstadt das im 14. Jahrhundert erbaute Schloß

Rapperswil au bord du lac de Zurich.
Construit au XIVᵉ siècle, le château
domine la vieille ville

Rapperswil on Lake Zurich. The
14th century castle high above the
old part of the town

43

44   Die Stadthalle von Winterthur   Le Théâtre municipal de Winterthur   The Municipal Hall of Winterthur

Dießenhofen am Rhein,
im Mittelalter freie Reichsstadt

Diessenhofen au bord du Rhin,
ville libre au Moyen Age

Diessenhofen on the Rhine was, in the
Middle Ages, an independent Imperial city

45

Eglisau,
ein altes Rheinbrückenstädtchen

Eglisau,
petite ville ancienne au bord du Rhin

Eglisau is a little old town at
one of the Rhine bridges

46

Viadukt der Eisenbahnlinie
Zürich – Schaffhausen bei Eglisau

Viaduc de la ligne de chemin de fer
Zurich-Schaffhouse près d'Eglisau

Railway viaduct near Eglisau on
the Zurich-Schaffhausen line

47

Als mächtigster Wasserfall Mittel-
europas stürzt der Rhein 20 Meter
tief bei Schaffhausen in sein Bett

A Schaffhouse, le Rhin fait un saut
de vingt mètres; c'est la chute la
plus importante d'Europe centrale

The greatest central-European waterfall
near Schaffhausen, where the Rhine
plunges down over 65 feet

Schaffhausen: Das Kastell Munot
(1564–1585) mit interessantem Rundbau

Schaffhouse: le «Munot»,
donjon du XVIᵉ siècle

View of the 16th-century Munot Castle
at Schaffhausen with a fine Round Tower

49

50   Das mittelalterliche Schloß Arbon   Château d'Arbon (lac de Constance)   Arbon Castle on Lake Constance

Das Rathaus in Steckborn am
Bodensee

L'Hôtel de Ville de Steckborn
(lac de Constance)

The Town Hall of Steckborn on
Lake Constance

51

52   Wildhaus, der beliebte Luftkurort
und Wintersportplatz, mit Säntis

La station climatique
de Wildhaus

Wildhaus, the popular winter-sports
and health-resort, with Säntis

Das Zwinglizimmer im Geburtshaus des Reformators in Wildhaus

La chambre du réformateur Ulrich Zwingli, dans sa maison natale de Wildhaus

The Zwingli Room in the house of the reformer's birth-place at Wildhaus

53

Rorschach am Bodensee, einst Hafenplatz für St. Gallen, heute eine aufstrebende Industriestadt

Rorschach, au bord du lac de Constance, était autrefois le port de Saint-Gall; aujourd'hui, c'est une ville industrielle en plein essor

Rorschach on Lake Constance, once the harbour of St. Gallen, today a thriving industrial town

St. Gallen: die Stiftskirche
(1756/66),
ein Meisterwerk des Barocks

Saint-Gall: la cathédrale
(1756–1766).
chef-d'œuvre du style baroque

At St. Gallen, the Collegiate Church,
built 1756 to 1766,
is a baroque masterpiece

Die prächtige Stiftsbibliothek in
der ehemaligen Benediktiner-Abtei
St. Gallen

La splendide bibliothèque de
l'ancienne abbaye bénédictine de
Saint-Gall

The Great Library of the
Benedictine Abbey at St. Gallen

Kunstvoller Erker am Haus
„Zum Greif" in St. Gallen

Un bel encorbellement de la maison
«Zum Greif», à Saint-Gall

The oriel of the "Griffin House"
at St. Gallen is a work of art

Wil, einst Sommerresidenz der
Fürstäbte von St. Gallen

Wil, autrefois résidence d'été
des prince-abbés de Saint-Gall

Wil, once the Summer Residence of
the Prince Abbots of St. Gallen

Schloß Sargans, malerisch gelegen, einst Sitz der das Rheintal beherrschenden eidgenössischen Landvögte

Site pittoresque dominant la vallée du Rhin, le château de Sargans était jadis le siège de la confédération des baillis

The delightfully situated Castle of Sargans was once the seat of the Swiss governors of the Rhine Valley

62 Amden, auf sonnigen Matten, hoch über dem Walensee Amden étalé au soleil, sur une terrasse dominant le lac de Walensee Amden above the Walensee stands amid sunny alpine meadows

Im Obertoggenburg:
Blick auf die Churfirsten

Dans le haut Toggenburg:
vue sur les Churfirsten

View towards the Churfirsten
at Obertoggenburg

Die Kantonshauptstadt Glarus mit
dem Vorder-Glärnisch (2331 m)

Glaris, chef-lieu de canton,
et le Vorder-Glärnisch (2331 m)

The cantonal capital of Glarus
with Vorder-Glärnisch (7,648 ft)

Bad Ragaz, wegen seiner Heilquellen
ein viel besuchter Kurort

Bad Ragaz, célèbre depuis des
siècles pour ses sources thermales

The springs of the spa of Ragaz
have been famous for centuries

Chur, das römische „Curia
Raetorum", an der Vereinigung
der Bündner Paßstraßen,
Hauptstadt von Graubünden

Coire, l'ancienne «Curia Raetorum»
des Romains, capitale du canton
des Grisons, est située à la croisée
des routes des cols

Chur, the "Curia Raetorum"
of the Romans and the capital
of the Grisons, lies at the junction
of the "Buendner" Pass roads

Das Tor zum Engadin: der alte
Grenzübergang Finstermünz

La porte de l'Engadine: vieux poste
frontière de Finstermünz

The gateway to the Engadine: the old
frontier crossing point at Finstermünz

67

Davos, bedeutender Wintersportplatz, bekannt als Heilstätte für
Lungenkrankheiten

Centre de sports d'hiver élégant, Davos est
également célèbre pour ses installations
où l'on soigne les affections pulmonaires

Davos, an important winter sports
centre and well-known as a health
resort for pulmonary diseases

Arosa (1740–1890 m), einer der höchstgelegenen Luftkurorte der Schweiz

Arosa (1740–1890 m) compte parmi les stations climatiques les plus élevées de Suisse

Arosa (5,710–6,200 ft), one of the highest climatic spas in Switzerland

Schloß Tarasp mit Piz Pisoc
(3173 m) im Engadin

Château de Tarasp, et Piz Pisoc
en Basse-Engadine

Tarasp Castle, with Piz Pisoc
(10,410 ft) in the Engadine

Bad Scuol/Schuls-Tarasp-Vulpera,
ein Fremdenverkehrszentrum und
bekanntes Heilbad

Scuol/Schuls-Tarasp-Vulpera est à
la fois centre touristique et station
thermale

Scuol/Schuls-Tarasp-Vulpera, a
tourist centre and a well-known
health-resort

Klosters, Luftkurort und
Wintersportplatz, im von der
Landquart durchflossenen
breiten Tal des Prätigau gelegen

Klosters est à la fois station climatique
et de sports d'hiver. La localité est
située dans la large vallée de Prätigau
qu'irrigue la rivière Landquart

Klosters, a climatic spa and
winter sports resort in the
broad valley of the Landquart
in the Prätigau region

Die Albula-Bahn verbindet das Engadin mit der Kantonshauptstadt Chur. Bei diesem Meisterstück der Eisenbahn-Baukunst werden auf 6 km Länge 416 m Höhenunterschied überwunden

La voie ferrée de l'Albula relie l'Engadine à Coire. Pour réaliser ce chef-d'œuvre de l'art ferroviaire, on a dû surmonter une dénivellation de 416 mètres sur une longueur de 6 kilomètres

The Albula Railway connects the Engadine with the capital of the Canton of Chur. This masterpiece of railway engineering climbs a rise of 1,365 feet in 3.75 miles

Zernez, an der Nordwestrampe der Ofenpaß-Straße und westlicher Zugang zum Schweizer National-park, mit Piz Linard (3410 m), höchster Berg der Silvretta

Zernez est voisin de la route conduisant au col de l'Ofen et constitue l'entrée du Parc National. A l'arrière-plan, le Piz Linard, point culminant du massif de la Silvretta

Zernez, on the north-west ramp of the Ofen Pass Road and the western entrance to the Swiss National Park. Piz Linard (11,188 ft) is the highest peak in the Silvretta Group

Dorfbrunnen in Guarda   La fontaine du village à Guarda   Village fountain at Guarda   75

Ardez (1435 m), mit der Ruine
Steinsberg gegen Flüela-Paß
gesehen

Ardez (1435 m) et les ruines de
Steinsberg; à l'arrière-plan, le col de
la Flüela

Ardez (4,708 ft) with the ruins
of Steinsberg, seen against
Flüela Pass

Am Dorfplatz von Zuoz steht dieser
alte Brunnen und das um 1600
erbaute Haus der Familie Planta

La place de Zuoz avec sa vieille
fontaine et la maison de la famille
Planta

The old fountain and the Plantas'
family home (c. 1600) stand on the
village square of Zuoz

77

78　Samedan (1782 m), an der weitesten Stelle des Hochtales gelegen, ist auch im Winter ein „sonniger Ort"

Situé à l'endroit le plus large de la vallée, Samedan (1782 m) est, également en hiver, un «lieu ensoleillé»

Samedan (5,847 ft), situated in the widest part of this high valley, is a "place in the sun" in winter, too

Blick von Muottas Muragl (2453 m),
dem Aussichtsbalkon des Engadins,
auf Celerina, St. Moritz mit
Corviglia und Piz Nair

De Muottas Muragl (2453 m),
la terrasse panoramique de
l'Engadine, le regard se perd vers
Celerina, St-Moritz et la Corviglia,
et enfin le Piz Nair

View from Muottas Muragl
(8,048 ft), the supreme belvedere in
the Engadine, looking towards
Celerina and St. Moritz, with
Corviglia and Piz Nair

79

Curling-Rinks in Pontresina
(1803 m), internationaler Wintersportplatz und als Kurort weit
bekannt

Piste de curling à Pontresina
(1803 m), centre international de
sports d'hiver et station climatique
recherchée

Curling rinks at Pontresina
(5,916 ft), an international winter-
sports centre, widely-known also
as a health resort

80

Bernina, Piz Palü und Bellavista
(3922 m) über dem Morteratsch-Gletscher
vom Weg zur Bovalhütte (2495 m)

Bernina, Piz Palü, Bellavista (3922 m) et
le glacier de Morteratsch vus du chemin
conduisant au refuge de Boval (2495 m)

View of Piz Palü and Bellavista (12,867 ft)
above the Morteratsch Glacier, from the
path to the Boval Hut (8,186 ft)

81

Die erhabene Bergwelt der
Bernina von der Fuorcla
Surlei (2670 m); Piz Bernina
mit Biancograt (4049 m),
Piz Scerscen (3971 m) und
Piz Roseg (3937 m)

Vu de la Fuorcla Surlei
(2670 m), le massif de la
Bernina apparaît dans toute
sa splendeur; Piz Bernina et
Crête Bianco (4049 m),
Piz Scerscen (3971 m) et
Piz Roseg (3937 m)

The magnificent alpine
galaxy of the Bernina from
the Fuorcla Surlej (8,760 ft),
Piz Bernina with Bianco
Crest (13,284 ft), Piz Scerscen
(13,029 ft) and Piz Roseg
(12,917 ft)

Im Skigebiet des Piz Lagalb
(2898 m) mit Blick über die
Diavolezzahütte (2973 m) zum
Piz Bernina mit Biancograt

Du Piz Lagalb (2898 m), sommet recherché
par les skieurs, on jouit d'une vue admirable
vers le refuge de Diavolezza (2973 m) et le
Piz Bernina avec la Crête Bianco

On the skiing slopes of Piz Lagalb
(9,508 ft) with a view over the
Diavolezza Hut (9,754 ft) to Piz
Bernina with its Bianco Crest

◀ Der Piz della Margna (3159 m),
Wahrzeichen des Oberengadins

Le Piz della Margna (3159 m),
symbole de la Haute-Engadine

The landmark of Upper Engadine,
Piz della Margna is 10,364 ft high

85

St. Moritz und der Piz Nair (3057 m),
ein Zentrum des Skisports und Treff-
punkt internationaler Prominenz

St-Moritz, centre de sports d'hiver
très mondain, et le Piz Nair
(3057 m)

St. Moritz and Piz Nair (10,029 ft),
a skiing centre and rendezvous for
international High Society

Weltbad St. Moritz (1856 m),
dessen Heilquellen schon Paracelsus
1539 rühmte

Les sources thermales de St-Moritz
ont déjà été louées par Paracelsus en
1539

The world-famous spa, St. Moritz,
whose healing waters were praised
by Paracelsus as early as in 1539

1948 war St. Moritz Austragungsort
der Olympischen Winterspiele

Die ganze Schönheit des Engadins
ist in diesem Bild eingefangen:
der Silser See mit Piz della Margna

St-Moritz vit se dérouler les Jeux
Olympiques d'hiver 1948

Cette vue sur le Silser See et le Piz
della Margna illustre toute la beauté
de l'Engadine

In 1948, St. Moritz was the arena
for the Winter Olympics

The quintessential beauty of the
Engadine is caught in this picture:
Lake Sils with Piz della Margna

90 Luftseilbahn Corviglia-Piz Nair
mit dem Steinbock, dem Symbol
Graubündens

Le téléphérique Corviglia-Piz Nair
et le bouquetin, symbole des
Grisons

The aerial cableway from Corviglia
to Piz Nair, with the ibex, the
symbol of the Canton of Grisons

Auf Corviglia (2486 m), dem Skigebiet von St. Moritz

La Corviglia (2486 m), paradis des
skieurs de St-Moritz

On Corviglia (8,156 ft), the skiing
grounds of St. Moritz

In 13 gutausgebauten Kehren führt
die Malojapaß-Straße hinab in das
von prächtigen Bergen umrahmte
Bergell

Maloja (1810 m) am Südende des
Silser Sees und die Berge des
Bergells. Segantini liegt hier
begraben

La route du col de la Maloja
descend en lacets vers Bergell,
localité entourée de sommets
majestueux

Maloja (1810 m) est situé à la pointe méri-
dionale du lac de Sils; à l'arrière-plan, les
sommets du massif de Bergell. C'est à
Maloja que repose le peintre Segantini

In 13 well-constructed bends the
Maloja Pass Road leads down
into the Bergell surrounded by
magnificent mountains

Maloja (5,938 ft) at the south end
of Lake Sils, where Segantini lies
buried, and the Bergell Mountains

Weit über den Palügletscher reicht
der Blick von der Alp Grüm

De l'Alp Grüm, le regard s'étend
loin au-delà du glacier de Palü

The view from Alp Grüm reaches
far across the Palü Glaciers

Poschiavo, ein in seiner Bauweise
italienisch anmutendes Städtchen,
Hauptort des Puschlav

Petite ville dont l'architecture manifeste
un caractère nettement italien, Poschiavo
est la principale localité de la région

Poschiavo, the chief town of the
Poschiavo District, whose architectural
style leans toward the Italian

97

Soglio (1058 m), malerisch auf einer Hangterrasse oberhalb des von der Mera durchflossenen Val Bregaglia gelegen

Soglio (1058 m), localité construite sur une terrasse dominant le val Bregaglia où coule la Mera

Soglio (3,471 ft), most picturesquely situated on a sloping terrace above the Val Bregaglia through which the Mera flows

Blick auf den 3307 m hohen
Piz Badile im Bergell

Le Piz Badile (3307 m), sommet
du massif de Bergell

View towards Piz Badile (10,850 ft)
in the Bergell

100

Bondo im Bergell (823 m) in
schöner Lage am Eingang zu dem
wilden Val Bondasca

Bondo en Bergell (823 m), site
pittoresque à l'entrée du sauvage
Val Bondasca

Bondo in the Bergell (2,900 ft) in
a lovely situation at the entrance
to the wild Val Bondasca

101

Die gewaltige Eiswelt am Fuße des Felsgipfels Crast Agüzza (3869 m)

Ces masses de glace s'étendent au pied du sommet rocheux Crast Agüzza (3869 m)

The enormous mass of ice at the foot of the craggy peaks of Crast Agüzza (12,695 ft)

„Das Silberschloß" –
Piz Palü-Ostgipfel in der
Bernina-Gruppe

«Das Silberschloß» – le château d'argent –
tel est le nom de la pointe orientale du
Piz Palü, sommet du massif de la Bernina

"The Silver Castle" – the
eastern peak of Piz Palü
in the Bernina Group

An solchen Erkern zeigt sich
der Form- und Farbensinn
der Engadiner

Ces ornements de la façade témoignent
du goût des formes et des couleurs
caractérisant les habitants de l'Engadine

The fine feeling for colour and form
typical of the Engadine people is
demonstrated by such oriel windows

Romanische Deckengemälde (11.Jh.)
in der St.-Martins-Kirche von Zillis

Le plafond décoré de l'église romane
Saint-Martin (XIe siècle) à Zillis

Romanesque ceiling (11th century)
in St. Martin's Church at Zillis ▶

Tiefencastel, ein wichtiger Straßen-
knotenpunkt am Zusammenfluß von
Albula und Julia

Tiefencastel, important nœud
routier au confluent de l'Albula
et de la Julia

Tiefencastel, an important
road-junction at the point
where Albula and Julia meet

Schloß Ortenstein im burgenreichen
Domleschg; in der Ferne Piz Beverin
(3002 m)

Le château Ortenstein, dans la vallée
du Domleschg. Dans le lointain, le
Piz Beverin (3002 m)

Ortenstein Castle, one of the
numerous castles of the Domleschg;
Piz Beverin in the distance (9,850 ft)

Splügen am Kreuzpunkt der
Straßen zum Splügen- (2118 m)
und San-Bernardino-Paß (2066 m)

Splügen, à la croisée des routes
du Splügen (2118 m) et du
San Bernardino (2066 m)

Splügen at the intersection of the
roads to the Splügen (6,949 ft)
and St. Bernard Pass (6,887 ft)

Die berühmte Felsenklamm
des Hinterrheins:
die Via Mala bei Thusis

La Via Mala, près de Thusis,
défilé célèbre où bouillonnent
les eaux du Rhin

The famous ravine of the Rhine
below the Via Mala near Thusis

Wild und ungebärdig zeigt sich der
Rhein in seinen Anfängen, hier der
Hinterrhein am Rheinwald

Sauvage et récalcitrant, deux caractères
du Rhin sur son cours supérieur.
Ici, le Rhin postérieur au Rheinwald

Not far from its sources, the Hinterrhein near Rheinwald presents
a scene of wild torrential waters

110

Im Vorderrheintal unterhalb
von Ilanz

Dans la vallée du Rhin antérieur,
en aval d'Ilanz

In the Valley of the Vorderrhein,
below Ilanz

111

112   Bern, Landes- und Kantonshauptstadt,   Berne, capitale fédérale et cantonale,   Berne and the Alps of the Bernese Oberland,
und die Alpen des Berner Oberlandes   et les Alpes de l'Oberland bernois   The city is both the Federal and Cantonal capital

Bern: das Münster, begonnen 1421,
gehört zu den bedeutendsten
gotischen Kirchen Europas

Berne: la Cathédrale, dont la construction
débuta en 1421, est l'un des plus impor-
tants monuments gothiques d'Europe

The Cathedral at Berne, begun in
1421, is one of the most important
Gothic churches in Europe

113

Thun, am Ausfluß der Aare
aus dem See, mit den Gipfeln
des Berner Oberlandes

Thoune, où l'Aar quitte le lac
sous l'œil grandiose des Alpes
de l'Oberland bernois

Thun. From where the Aar leaves
the lake, one can see the peaks
of the Bernese Oberland

116

Spiez am Thuner See, bedeutender
Luftkur- und Erholungsort

Le château de Spiez, au milieu d'un
paysage enchanteur

Spiez Castle amid an enchanting
landscape, a climatic resort

118   Der Weltkurort Interlaken   Interlaken, station de villégiature des plus répu-   Interlaken, an international resort,
mit Jungfrau und Eiger   tées de Suisse, dominée par l'Eiger et la Jungfrau   with the Eiger and Jungfrau Peaks

Blick von Brünig-Hasliberg auf
Wetterhorn, Mönch und Eiger

Vue depuis le Brünig-Hasliberg sur
le Wetterhorn, le Mönch et l'Eiger

View from Brünig-Hasliberg towards
Wetterhorn, Mönch and Eiger peaks

119

122   Motiv im „Gletscherdorf" Grindelwald   Grindelwald: motif du «village-glacier»   A scene in the "glacier-village" of Grindelwald

Blick von Brünig-Hasliberg auf
Wetterhorn, Mönch und Eiger

Vue depuis le Brünig-Hasliberg sur
le Wetterhorn, le Mönch et l'Eiger

View from Brünig-Hasliberg towards
Wetterhorn, Mönch and Eiger peaks

119

Hier ist die ganze Majestät des Berner
Oberlandes eingefangen: das Tal von
Lauterbrunnen mit dem gewaltigen Tal-
schluß; vorn auf der Terrasse Wengen, unten
im Talgrund Lauterbrunnen.,
rechts der Staubbachfall; im Hintergrund
Mittaghorn, Breithorn, Tschingelhorn,
Tschingelspitz und Gspaltenhorn

L'Oberland bernois dans toute sa splendeur:
la vallée de Lauterbrunnen tout entière; sur la
terrasse au premier plan, le village de Wengen;
plus bas, le village de Lauterbrunnen; à
droite, la cascade du Staubbach. A l'arrière-
plan, Mittaghorn, Breithorn, Tschingelhorn,
pic du Tschingel et Gspaltenhorn

The sublime majesty of the Bernese Oberland
is here revealed. The Valley of Lauterbrunnen with its mighty barrier; Wengen
lies on the terrace in the foreground, and in
the valley, Lauterbrunnen. On the right
Staubbach Falls; in the background,
Mittaghorn, Breithorn, Tschingelhorn,
Tschingelspitz and Gspaltenhorn

122   Motiv im „Gletscherdorf" Grindelwald   Grindelwald: motif du «village-glacier»   A scene in the "glacier-village" of Grindelwald

Die Kleine Scheidegg (2064 m)
am Fuß der gewaltigen
Eiger-Nordwand (3974 m)

La petite Scheidegg (2064 m)
au pied de l'imposante paroi nord
de l'Eiger (3974 m)

Kleine Scheidegg (6,772 ft) at the
foot of the mighty Eiger North Wall
(13,042 ft)

Durch eine grandiose
Landschaft führt die
Jungfraubahn zum
höchsten Bahnhof
Europas in 3454 m
Höhe. – Jungfrau,
Schneehorn
und Silberhorn

Le funiculaire «Jung-
fraubahn» traverse un
paysage grandiose
avant d'atteindre le
terminus à 3454 mètres.
Jungfrau, Schneehorn
et Silberhorn

The Jungfrau Railway
passes through
magnificent scenery on
the way to the highest
station in Europe at
11,332 ft. Jungfrau,
Schneehorn
and Silberhorn

Station Birg der Schilt-
horn-Bahn mit Eiger,
Mönch und Jungfrau

La station Birg du
train du Schilthorn
avec l'Eiger, le Mönch
et la Jungfrau

Birg Station on the
Schilthorn Rly. with
Eiger, Mönch and
Jungfrau in view

126   Käseteilet im Justistal   La répartition des fromages, dans le Justistal   "Käseteilet", dividing the cheeses, in Justistal

Der Grimselstausee und das Grimselhospiz;
der angestaute See ist über 5 km lang

Le lac artificiel du Grimsel, d'une
longueur de 5 km, et l'hospice

The Grimsel Dam and the Hospice;
the water stretches back well over 3 mls.   127

Alphornbläser auf dem Männlichen

Les joueurs de cor des Alpes au Männlichen

Alpine-horn blowers on the Männlichen

128

Im Männlichengebiet mit Mönch, Tschuggen und Jungfrau

Dans la plaine du Männlichen. Au fond Mönch, Tschuggen et Jungfrau

In the Männlichen District. Mönch, Tschuggen and Jungfrau

129

Adelboden, vielbesuchter Luftkurort und Wintersportplatz

Adelboden, station thermale et de
sports d'hiver très fréquentée

Adelboden, a much frequented
climatic and winter-sports resort

Kandersteg, überragt von Wildstrubel, Tschingellochtighorn und
Großer und Kleiner Lohner

Kandersteg d'où l'on voit le Wildstrubel, le Tschingellochtighorn,
le grand et le petit Lohner

Wildstrubel, Tschingellochtighorn
and Großer and Kleiner Lohner
tower above Kandersteg

131

Standseilbahn Mürren–Allmendhubel, im Hintergrund das
Lauterbrunner Breithorn (3782 m)

Le chemin de fer à crémaillère
Mürren–Allmendhubel; au fond
le Breithorn (3782 m)

Mürren–Allmendhubel Funicular
Railway, with Breithorn (12,408 ft)
in the background

Lenk im weiten Talgrund des
Simmentales. Dorfstraße
und der beliebte Eissport Curling

La Lenk, au fond de la vallée du Simmen-
tal. La rue principale du village et la
patinoire avec ses joueurs de curling

Lenk in the wide valley of the
Simmen. The village street and
the popular ice-sport, curling

132

Gstaad, Wohnort der Prominenz,
mit Wildhorn, Geltengletscher und
Windspielen

Gstaad, lieu de promenades. Dans le
fond, le Wildhorn, le glacier Gelten
et le Windspielen

At Gstaad, where celebrities meet,
Wildhorn, Gelten Glacier and
Windspielen in the background

Der Oeschinensee (1578 m) unterhalb der Blümlisalpgruppe (3664 m),
ein Glanzpunkt der Berner Alpen

Le lac d'Oeschinen situé à 1578 mètres,
est dominé par la Blümlisalp (3664 m), l'un
des plus jolis sommets des Alpes Bernoises

Lake Oeschinen (5,177 ft) below the
Blümlisalp Group (12,021 ft) a
highlight in the Bernese Alps

Andermatt, ein bekannter Wintersportplatz, im Herzen der Zentralschweiz gelegen

Andermatt, célèbre station de sports d'hiver en Suisse centrale

Andermatt, a well-known winter-sports resort, lies in the heart of central Switzerland

Göschenen, an der Einfahrt zum
15 km langen Gotthardtunnel

Göschenen, à l'entrée du tunnel
du St-Gothard, long de 15 km

Göschenen at the entrance to the
10-mile-long St. Gotthard Tunnel

137

Bürgelen, an der Straße zum
Klausenpaß, nach der Überlieferung
Heimatort Wilhelm Tells

Bürgelen sur la route du col du
Klausen. Selon la légende, c'est la
patrie de Tell

Bürgelen, on the road to the Klausen
Pass, was Tell's birthplace, tradition
says

Flüelen am Urner See
mit Bristenstock (3074 m)

Flüelen au bord du lac d'Uri
et le Bristenstock (3074 m)

Flüelen on Lake Urn,
with Bristenstock (10,085 ft.)

142   Blick von der Hegmatt auf das   Vue de la Hegmatt sur le village   Looking down from Hegmatt to the
       verschneite Klosterdorf Engelberg   d'Engelberg avec son cloître et les   monastic village of Engelberg, here in
       mit Hahnen (2606 m)   Hahnen (2606 m)   snow. Mount Hahnen rises to 8,550 ft

Bürgelen, an der Straße zum
Klausenpaß, nach der Überlieferung
Heimatort Wilhelm Tells

Bürgelen sur la route du col du
Klausen. Selon la légende, c'est la
patrie de Tell

Bürgelen, on the road to the Klausen
Pass, was Tell's birthplace, tradition
says

Flüelen am Urner See
mit Bristenstock (3074 m)

Flüelen au bord du lac d'Uri
et le Bristenstock (3074 m)

Flüelen on Lake Urn,
with Bristenstock (10,085 ft.)

Blick von der Hegmatt auf das verschneite Klosterdorf Engelberg mit Hahnen (2606 m)

Vue de la Hegmatt sur le village d'Engelberg avec son cloître et les Hahnen (2606 m)

Looking down from Hegmatt to the monastic village of Engelberg, here in snow. Mount Hahnen rises to 8,550 ft

Bürgelen, an der Straße zum
Klausenpaß, nach der Überlieferung
Heimatort Wilhelm Tells

Bürgelen sur la route du col du
Klausen. Selon la légende, c'est la
patrie de Tell

Bürgelen, on the road to the Klausen
Pass, was Tell's birthplace, tradition
says

Flüelen am Urner See
mit Bristenstock (3074 m)

Flüelen au bord du lac d'Uri
et le Bristenstock (3074 m)

Flüelen on Lake Urn,
with Bristenstock (10,085 ft.)

Altdorf, Hauptort des Kantons Uri, mit vielen Zeugen der Vergangenheit, eines der freundlichsten Landstädtchen in der Schweiz

Altdorf est le chef-lieu du canton d'Uri. Avec ses nombreux témoignages du passé, c'est une des villes les plus accueillantes de Suisse

Altdorf, the cantonal capital of Uri, one of the pleasantest little country towns in Switzerland, still preserves much evidence of its past

Brunnen – an der Gotthardroute –
berühmter Kurort in sonniger Bucht
am See

Brunnen, sur la route du Gothard,
est un lieu de vacances renommé
dans une baie ensoleillée

Brunnen on the St. Gotthard Route,
a famous health-resort on a sunny
bay in the Lake

Blick von der Hegmatt auf das verschneite Klosterdorf Engelberg mit Hahnen (2606 m)

Vue de la Hegmatt sur le village d'Engelberg avec son cloître et les Hahnen (2606 m)

Looking down from Hegmatt to the monastic village of Engelberg, here in snow. Mount Hahnen rises to 8,550 ft

Rütliwiese, Geburtsstätte der Schweiz. „Hier standen die Väter zusammen für Freiheit und heimisches Gut"

Prairie du Rütli. Nous sommes au cœur de la Suisse. «Ici se retrouvèrent nos ancêtres pour la liberté et le bien du pays»

"Rütliwiese", the birthplace of Switzerland. "Here our forefathers made a stand for freedom and our common heritage"

Föhnsturm über dem Urner See   Sur le lac d'Uri, quand le fœhn   Southerly storm (Foehn) over Lake Urn

souffle en tempête

144

Das alte Schifferhaus „Zur Treib",
bereits 1482 urkundlich erwähnt

La vieille maison des bateliers
à Treib date de 1482

The ancient boatman's inn, "Zur Treib"
mentioned in documents as early as 1482

Gersau, liebliches Dorf am See,
während fünf Jahrhunderten die
146 kleinste Republik der Welt

Gersau, charmant village au bord du
lac, a été pendant cinq siècles la plus
petite république du monde

Gersau, a lovely village on the Lake,
was the tiniest republic in the world
for five centuries

Hotel Engel in Küßnacht am Rigi,
eine alte Gaststätte, in der schon
Goethe 1775 einkehrte

L'hôtel Engel à Küssnacht au pied
du Rigi. Cette ancienne hôtellerie
accueillit Goethe en 1775

Hotel Engel (The Angel) at Küssnacht on the Rigi, an ancient inn
at which Goethe stayed in 1775

147

Die kühnangelegte Autobahn Luzern-Stans zwischen Vierwaldstätter See und Lopper/Zentralschweiz. Im Hintergrund der Pilatus

L'autoroute Lucerne-Stans déroule son ruban hardi entre le lac des Quatre-Cantons et le promontoire du Lopper/Suisse centrale. A l'arrière-plan, le Pilate

The boldly constructed throughway Lucerne-Stans between the Lake of Four Cantons and Lopper/Central Switzerland

Blick vom Pilatus über den
Bürgenstock auf die Berge der
Zentralschweiz

Vue du Pilate au-delà du Bürgenstock vers les montagnes de la Suisse
centrale

View from Pilatus over the
Bürgenstock towards the mountains
of central Switzerland

149

Am rechten Ufer der Reuß die Luzerner Altstadt, in der noch Bürgerhäuser des 16. und 17. Jh.s erhalten sind

Sur la rive droite de la Reuss, la vieille ville de Lucerne avec ses maisons patriciennes des XVIe et XVIIe siècles

The right bank of the Reuss is where the old burghers' houses of the 16th and 17th centuries still stand in the Old Quarter of Lucerne

150 Luzern: Kantonshauptstadt und Mittelpunkt des Schweizer Fremdenverkehrs

Lucerne: chef-lieu du canton et principal centre touristique Suisse

Lucerne, the cantonal capital and chief centre for Swiss tourism ▶

Die Benediktiner-Abtei Einsiedeln, 934 gegründet, berühmtester Wallfahrtsort der Schweiz

Einsiedeln, abbaye bénédictine fondé en 934, est le principal lieu de pèlerinage existant en Suisse

The Benedictine Abbey at Einsiedeln, founded in 934, is the most famous place of pilgrimage in Switzerland

Zug, Hauptstadt des gleichnamigen Kantons: Kolinplatz   La place Kolin à Zoug   On Kolin Square at Zug   153

Schwyz: das bemalte Rathaus
der Kantonshauptstadt wurde 1642
bis 1645 erbaut.

154   Im Hintergrund der Große Mythen

Schwytz: l'Hôtel de Ville du chef-
lieu a été construit de 1642 à 1645.
A l'arrière-plan, le grand Mythen

The painted Town Hall of Schwyz,
the cantonal capital, was built
between 1642 and 1645.
The Great Mythen in the background

Der Landsknechtsturm in Sempach   La Tour du Lansquenet à Sempach   The Mercenary's Tower at Sempach   155

Solothurn, eine alte Stadt am Fuße des Jura

Soleure: une vieille cité au pied du Jura

Solothurn, at the foot of the Jura

Moutier im Münstertal,
Kanton Bern

Moutier, dans le Jura bernois

Moutier in the Münster Valley,
Canton of Berne

157

158 Delémont: Brunnen in der Altstadt aus dem 16. Jahrhundert

Delémont: dans la vieille ville, une fontaine du XVIe siècle

Delémont: 16th-cent. fountain in the old quarter

Porrentruy: altes Städtchen
an der Allaine (Uhrenindustrie)

Porrentruy: ancienne petite ville
horlogère sur les rives de l'Allaine

Porrentruy, an ancient townlet on
the Allaine, engaged in watchmaking

160   Malerischer Altstadtwinkel in Biel   Aspect pittoresque du Vieux-Bienne   A pleasing corner in the old part of Biel

Ligerz am Bieler See und die
St. Petersinsel, Kanton Bern

Gléresse, sur les rives du lac
de Bienne, et l'île Saint-Pierre

Ligerz on Bielersee and Peter's Island,
Canton of Berne

161

Der Doubs bei Les Brenets   Le Doubs près Les Brenets,   The Doubs River at Les Brenets,

162   an der französischen Grenze   à la frontière française   on the French frontier

St. Ursanne, malerisch eingebettet
in einer Schleife des Doubs

Saint-Ursanne se dresse pittoresque-
ment dans l'une des boucles du Doubs

Picturesque St. Ursanne, situated
on a loop of the Doubs River

La Chaux-de-Fonds, Mittelpunkt
164 der 1705 eingeführten Uhrenindustrie

La Chaux-de-Fonds, centre de l'industrie horlogère établie depuis 1705

La Chaux-de-Fonds is the hub of the
watch industry established in 1705

Le Locle, ein Hauptort
der Schweizer Uhrenindustrie

Le Locle, l'une des métropoles
horlogères de la Suisse

Le Locle, a centre of the Swiss
watch industry

In den Weinbergen am See
von Neuchâtel

Dans les vignobles qui dominent
le lac de Neuchâtel

In the vineyards on the slopes
above Lake Neuchâtel

◀ Die Felsenschlucht
Gorges de l'Areuse

Les Gorges de l'Areuse,
près de Neuchâtel

"Gorges de l'Areuse"
at Neuchâtel

Neuchâtel: die ehemalige
Markthalle, 1570 erbaut

Neuchâtel: les anciennes Halles,
construites en 1570

Neuchâtel: the old Fruit and
Vegetable Market, built 1570

168

Murten am See, interessantes Städtchen
mit alter Mauer und Wehrgang

Dans la petite et pittoresque cité
médiévale de Morat

In ancient, picturesque Murten

170   Fribourg, alte Bischofs- und   Fribourg, vieille ville épiscopale   Fribourg, an ancient city with University
Universitätsstadt an der Saane   et universitaire, sur la Sarine   and bishop, is on the River Sarine

Fribourg: Das alte Rathaus und die
Kathedrale St. Nicolas

Fribourg: l'ancien Hôtel de Ville
et la cathédrale St-Nicolas

The ancient Town Hall of Fribourg
and the Cathedral of St. Nicolas

171

172   Beim Großvater in einem Greyerzer   La lecture de l'aïeul, dans une ferme   In a Greyerz farm-house, children
       Bauernhaus   de la Gruyère   listen to grandfather's stories

Schloß Gruyères
in der gleichnamigen Landschaft

Le château de Gruyères domine une
région de pâturages fertiles

Gruyères Castle and country-side

Yverdon: das Schloß der Herzöge
von Savoyen aus dem 13. Jahrh.

Yverdon: le château des ducs de
Savoie, construit au XIIIe siècle

At Yverdon, the 13th-cent. castle
of the Dukes of Savoy

Römische Ausgrabungen in Nyon
am Genfer See

Fouilles romaines à Nyon, sur les
rives du lac Léman

Excavated Roman remains at
Nyon on Lake Geneva

176   Morges: Blick in die Grand-Rue   Morges: coup d'œil sur la Grand-Rue   Morges' Grand-Rue

Der bekannte Weinort
St. Saphorin mit der Kirche aus
dem 16. Jahrhundert

Saint-Saphorin, dont le vin
est réputé, avec son église du
XVIᵉ siècle

St. Saphorin,
with its 16th-cent. church, is
famous for wine

Genf: das Völkerbundspalais, heute
Sitz der Vereinten Nationen in Europa

Genève: devant le Palais des
Nations

Geneva's centre for international politics,
now the U. N. European Headquaters

Genf, Universitätsstadt und Tagungsort
internationaler Institutionen

Genève, ville universitaire et siège
d'institutions internationales

Geneva, a university-town and the scene of
many congresses of international institutions

„Jet d'eau", die 120 m hohe
Wasserfontäne im See vor Genf,
Wahrzeichen der Stadt

Le Jet d'eau, qui atteint 120 m,
une des caractéristiques
de Genève

"Jet d'eau", the jet of water
springing 394 ft. above Lake
Geneva, is the town's landmark

Die Kathedrale von Lausanne,
1275 von Papst Gregor X. geweiht

La cathédrale de Lausanne, consacrée
en 1275 par le pape Grégoire X

The Cathedral of Lausanne, con-
secrated by Pope Gregory X in 1275

181

Lausanne am Genfer See. Blick auf den Grand-Pont und die Altstadt

Lausanne sur le lac Léman. Vue sur le Grand-Pont et la vieille ville

Lausanne on Lake Geneva. View of the Grand-Pont and the old part of the city

182

Lausanne: Place St. François
mit gleichnamiger Kirche

Lausanne: La place Saint-François,
avec l'église du même nom

Lausanne, the Square and the
Church of St. François

Kurort Montreux, in prachtvoller
Lage mit ungewöhnlich mildem
Klima, am Genfer See.
Schwimmbad des Casinos

Montreux est une station
climatique recherchée; elle jouit
d'un site magnifique et d'un climat
très agréable. Ici, la piscine du
Casino

The health resort of Montreux is
situated in a splendid position on
Lake Geneva and has an unusually
mild climate. The Casino
swimming-pool

Lausanne: Place St. François
mit gleichnamiger Kirche

Lausanne: La place Saint-François,
avec l'église du même nom

Lausanne, the Square and the
Church of St. François

Kurort Montreux, in prachtvoller
Lage mit ungewöhnlich mildem
Klima, am Genfer See.
Schwimmbad des Casinos

Montreux est une station
climatique recherchée; elle jouit
d'un site magnifique et d'un climat
très agréable. Ici, la piscine du
Casino

The health resort of Montreux is
situated in a splendid position on
Lake Geneva and has an unusually
mild climate. The Casino
swimming-pool

Lausanne: Place St. François
mit gleichnamiger Kirche

Lausanne: La place Saint-François,
avec l'église du même nom

Lausanne, the Square and the
Church of St. François

183

Weinberge, soweit das Auge reicht. Hier bei Lutry ...

Des vignobles à perte de vue. Ici, près de Lutry ...

Vineyards everywhere. These are near Lutry ...

... und ein paar Kilometer weiter Weinlese bei Rivaz

... et, quelques kilomètres plus loin, les vendanges près de Rivaz

... and a few miles away, the vintage at Rivaz

Kurort Montreux, in prachtvoller
Lage mit ungewöhnlich mildem
Klima, am Genfer See.
Schwimmbad des Casinos

Montreux est une station
climatique recherchée; elle jouit
d'un site magnifique et d'un climat
très agréable. Ici, la piscine du
Casino

The health resort of Montreux is
situated in a splendid position on
Lake Geneva and has an unusually
mild climate. The Casino
swimming-pool

Blick auf Vevey mit dem Genfer See   Vue sur Vevey et le lac Léman   View of Vevey on Lake Geneva   187

188   Blick über die Rochers de Naye (2045 m)   Vue sur les Rochers de Naye (2045 m)   Aerial view of Rochers de Naye

Am oberen Ende des Val d'Illiez,
unterhalb der siebenzackigen
Dents du Midi, liegt der Luftkurort und Wintersportplatz
Champéry

Au-dessous des Dents du Midi,
groupe composé de sept dents,
se blottit Champéry, station
climatique et centre de sports
d'hiver du haut val d'Illiez

At the upper end of the Illiez Valley
and below the seven jagged peaks of
the Dents du Midi lies Champéry,
a mountain health-resort and
winter-sports centre

189

Das burgartige Schloß Aigle, bis
1798 Sitz der bernischen Landvögte

Le château d'Aigle fut jusqu'en 1798
la résidence des baillis bernois

The turreted Aigle Castle, till 1798
the seat of the governors of Berne

Schloß Chillon am Genfer See, eine
alte Burg der Herzöge von Savoyen

Le château de Chillon, l'antique
bourg des ducs de Savoie, fut construit dès le IXe siècle

Chillon Castle on the Lake of
Geneva is the ancestral castle of the
Dukes of Savoy

191

Der Engpaß von St. Maurice, die ,,Pforte zum Wallis", spielte schon zur Römerzeit als Zollposten eine wichtige Rolle. Das Schloß wurde 1523 erbaut

St-Maurice, la «Porte du Valais», était déjà un poste de douane important à l'époque romaine, Le château date de 1523.

The bottleneck at St. Maurice, the "Gateway to Valais", played an important role as a customs barrier even in Roman times. The Castle dates from 1523

Die Paßstraße über den Col de la
Forclas (1527 m) verbindet das Rhônetal
mit dem Hochtal von Chamonix

La route du Col de la Forclaz
(1527 m) relie la vallée du Rhône
à la haute-vallée de Chamonix

The road over the Col de la Forclas
(5,010 ft) connects the Rhône Valley
with the alpine valley of Chamonix

193

Martigny, Kreuzungspunkt internationaler Alpenstraßen, an der
Mündung der Drance in die Rhône
gelegene alte Stadt, dessen Wahrzeichen der Turm von Bâtiaz ist

La tour de Bâtiaz est le signe
caractéristique de Martigny, localité
située au confluent de la Drance et
du Rhône, et point d'intersection de
routes transalpines internationales

Martigny, where international
alpine routes intersect, is an old
town at the confluence of the
Drance and the Rhône. The Tower
of Bâtiaz is its landmark

Fionnay und der Mont Pleureur
(3703 m). Am Ende des Bagnestales
beginnt der große Stausee von
Mauvoisin

Fionnay et le Mont Pleureur
(3703 m). Dans le haut val de
Bagnes commence le grand lac du
Barrage de Mauvoisin

Fionnay and Mt. Pleureur
(12,149 ft). The great Mauvoisin
Dam stands at the end of the
Bagnes Valley

195

Aiguilles Dorées im Trientgebiet,
darüber erhebt sich der Grand
Combin

Les Aiguilles Dorées dans la zone du
Trient; derrière, le Grand Combin

The Aiguilles Dorées in the Trient
District, beyond which the Grand
Combin soars up

Großer St. Bernhard (2473 m), ein seit dem Altertum benutzter Paß auf dem Hauptkamm der Alpen mit dem berühmten Hospiz

Col de la crête principale des Alpes, le Grand St-Bernard (2473 m) est utilisé depuis l'antiquité. Son hospice célèbre

The Great St. Bernhard (8,114 ft) has been a pass over the chief dividing range of the Alps since the days of antiquity. Here is also the famous Hospice

197

Bekannte Walliser Weine wachsen
in den Weinbergen bei Saillon

Ces vignobles des environs de
Saillon produisent les vins cotés du
Valais

Well-known Valais wines are
produced in the terraced vineyards
near Saillon

Hoch droben auf saftigen Berg-
wiesen im Val d'Hérens liegt
La Forclaz (1700 m)

Perché au milieu d'alpages
verdoyants, La Forclaz (1700 m),
pittoresque village du Val d'Hérens

The village of La Forclaz (5,577 ft)
lies high up in the lush mountain
pastures of the Hérens Valley

199

Die Erdpyramiden von Euseigne, die vor Jahrtausenden aus dem eiszeitlichen Moränenschutt ausgewaschen wurden

Les pyramides de terre d'Euseigne sont les restes d'anciennes moraines

The pyramids of earth washed out of ice-age moraines thousands of years ago, at Euseigne

Blick von Verbier auf die
schneebedeckte Grand-Combin-
Gruppe

De Verbier, on voit étinceler au
soleil la neige recouvrant le massif
du Grand Combin

Panorama of the snow-clad Grand-
Combin Range seen from Verbier

201

Crans sur Sierre (1500 m) ein moderner
Kurort und bedeutender Wintersport-
platz auf einem weiten sonnigen nach
Süden geneigten Hochplateau

Crans sur Sierre (1500 m) est une station climatique moderne et un important centre de sports
d'hiver; exposé au sud, le vaste haut-plateau en
pente douce est longtemps ensoleillé

Crans sur Sierre (4,921 ft), a modern
health-resort and an important
winter-sports centre on a wide sunny
plateau sloping southwards

Montana-Vermala, Kurort und
Sportzentrum ersten Ranges, im
Herzen der Walliser Alpen in einer
Höhenlage von 1500 Metern

Montana-Vermala, station climatique
et centre de sports d'hiver de premier
ordre, au cœur des Alpes Valaisannes,
à 1500 mètres d'altitude

Montana-Vermala, a health-resort
and sports centre of top rank in the
heart of the Valais Alps, lies at an
altitude of 4,921 ft

Sion/Sitten, am Fuße der Burghügel
Valère und Tourbillon, Hauptstadt
des Kantons Wallis, Regierungs-
und Bischofssitz

Au pied des collines Valère et
Tourbillon s'étend Sion, capitale
du Valais, siège du gouvernement
et siège épiscopal

Sion/Sitten, at the foot of the hills crowned
by the Castles of Valère and Tourbillon,
is the capital of the Canton of Valais, the
seat of a bishop and of the administration

Eine in den Fels gehauene Straße
führt nach St. Luc im Val d'Anniviers

Cette route en corniche conduit à
St-Luc dans le Val d'Anniviers

A road hewn out of the rock-face
leads to St. Luc in the Anniviers Valley

Die Herrgottsgrenadiere von
Kippel beim „Segensonntag" im
Lötschental

Les grenadiers de Kippel dans le
Lötschental pendant la cérémonie
du «Segensonntag»

The "Grenadiers of the Lord God"
of Kippel in Lötschental on
Benediction Sunday

Grimentz (1570 m) im Val d'Anniviers, ein Schmuckstück der Walliser Dörfer, mit Häusern aus weißgetünchtem Stein und sonnengebranntem Holz

Grimentz (1570 m) dans le Val d'Anniviers, typique village valaisan aux maisons en pierre blanchie à la chaux et dont les parties en bois sont brûlées par le soleil

Grimentz (5,151 ft) in the Anniviers Valley, is a jewel among the Valais villages, with its houses of whitewashed stone and sunbrowned timber

Leukerbad, das schon die Römer
schätzten und Goethe rühmte, ist
heute das bedeutendste Thermal-
heilbad der Schweiz

Déjà apprécié des romains et vanté
par Goethe, Loèche-les-Bains est
aujourd'hui la première station
thermale suisse

Leukerbad, esteemed by the
Romans and extolled by Goethe,
is the most important thermal spa
in Switzerland today

Der Große Aletschgletscher, mit 24 km Gesamtlänge, größter Eisstrom der Alpen

Avec ses 24 km de longueur totale, le grand glacier d'Aletsch est le plus long d'Europe

The Great Aletsch Glacier with a total length of 15 miles is the longest stream of ice in the Alps

Brig, Hauptort des Oberwallis, Kreuzungspunkt internationaler Verkehrswege. Im Hintergrund die Belalp

Brigue, principale localité du Haut-Valais, est un nœud de communications important. A l'arrière-plan, le Belalp

Brig, the chief town in Upper Valais, lies at the intersection of international routes. In the background, the Belalp (7,011 ft)

Visp, an der Mündung der Visp in
die Rhône gelegenes Städtchen mit
lebhafter Industrie

Viège, localité située au confluent de
la Viège et du Rhône, est le siège
d'industries prospères

Visp, situated at the confluence of
the Visp and the Rhône, is a busy
little industrial town

Aus dem kleinen Pfarrdorf Niederwald
zog César Ritz in die Welt hinaus –
Begründer der weltberühmten Ritz-Hotels

César Ritz – le fondateur des
célèbres hôtels Ritz – est originaire
du petit village de Niederwald

From this little parish, Niederwald,
César Ritz went out into the world
to found the famous Ritz hotels

Gletsch (1761) mit Galenstock (3597 m) und Rhônegletscher aus dem die Rhône ihren Anfang nimmt

Gletsch (1761 m) est dominé par le Galenstock (3597 m) et le glacier du Rhône, ainsi appelé car c'est là que naît le fleuve

Gletsch (5,778 ft) with Galenstock (11,801 ft) and the Rhône Glacier, from which the Rhône springs

213

Das Bergdorf Grächen (1617 m) mit der Hannigalp (2110 m), einem bekannten Skigebiet

Grächen, village situé à 1617 mètres et dominé par le Hannigalp (2110 m), montagne recherchée des skieurs

The mountain village of Grächen (5,305 ft) and the Hannigalp (6,923 ft), a well-known skiing ground

Unterhalb des Riedgletschers und des Nadelhorns steht das eigenartige Kirchlein von Ried, unweit von St. Niklaus

Au pied du glacier de Ried et du Nadelhorn se dresse la bizarre petite église de Ried, non loin de St-Nicolas

Below the Ried Glacier and the Nadel Ridge stands the singular little chapel of Ried, not far from St. Niklaus

Blick vom Gornergrat auf die Dent Blanche, einem mächtigen Viertausender im westlichen Teil des großen Eiszirkus von Zermatt und auf das stolze Obergabelhorn (rechts)

La Dent Blanche, imposant quatre mille s'élevant à l'ouest du cirque glaciaire de Zermatt, et le fier Obergabelhorn (à droite) vus du Gornergrat

View from the Gorner Ridge towards the Dent Blanche, one of the mightiest of the 13,000-ft mountains in the western part of the great Zermatt "ice circus" and towards the proud peak on the right, Obergabelhorn

Zermatt, der Kurort ohne Autos.
Handkarren und Pferdedroschken
sind die einzigen „Verkehrsmittel".
Das sonnige Matterhorndorf,
erhabenes Reiseziel der Welt –
anerkanntes Zentrum des Hoch-
gebirges

A Zermatt, on ne rencontre pas
d'autos. Diligences et fiacres sont
les seuls moyens de transports.
Le village ensoleillé blotti au pied
du Cervin, est une station de
haute montagne où règne une
ambiance mondaine

Zermatt, the health-resort without motor-
cars; the only means of transport here are
horse-drawn carriages and hand-carts.
The sunny village below the Matterhorn,
is the acknowledged centre for the
High Alps and the grand destination of
world-travellers

Monte Rosa: Die Dufourspitze, mit 4634 m höchster Gipfel der Schweiz

Monte Rosa: La Pointe Dufour (4634 m), le plus haut sommet de Suisse

Monte Rosa: Dufour Peak (15,217 ft) is the highest summit in Switzerland

Die gewaltigen Eisströme des
Theodul- und des Gornergletschers

Les imposants fleuves de glace des
glaciers de Theodul et du Gorner

These gigantic streams of ice are the
Theodul and the Gorner Glaciers

Dorf Simplon an der 1801 – 1805
auf Befehl Napoleons I. erbauten
Simplon-Straße über den Zentral-
kamm der Alpen

Le village de Simplon sur la route
du même nom aménagée de 1801 à
1805 sur l'ordre de Napoléon, sur la
crête centrale des Alpes

The village of Simplon (4,843 ft) lies on the
Simplon Road over the central ridge of
the Alps. The road was built by order of
Napoleon I between 1801 and 1805

Wie Filigran wirken die gigantischen Brücken der Lötschbergbahn – ein Meisterwerk menschlichen Planens

Chefs-d'œuvre dus à l'homme, les gigantesques viaducs de la ligne du Lötschberg ressemblent, dans ce paysage grandiose, à un filigrane

The gigantic viaducts of the Lötschberg Railway – a masterpiece of man's design – look like filigree work, as this does in the Bietsch Valley

Vorfrühlingsstimmung in den Saaser
Bergen

Prémices printaniers dans les
montagnes de Saas

Indications of early spring in the
Saas Mountains

Saas-Fee, die ,,Perle der Alpen"
genannt. Ein schmuckes Bergdorf
im Herzen der höchsten
Schweizer Berge

Saas-Fée, la «perle des Alpes».
Un coquet village de montagne
au cœur des Alpes suisses

Saas-Fee is known as the "Pearl
of the Alps". It is a pretty mountain
village in the heart of the highest
Swiss mountains

Bellinzona, Hauptstadt des Kantons Tessin, alte Festungsstadt an der St.-Gotthard- und der San-Bernardino-Paßstraße

Près de Bellinzone, la vieille forteresse helvétique, la route du Lukmanier rejoint celles qui viennent du Saint-Gothard et du San Bernardino

Bellinzona, the ancient Ticino fortress. The road joins that coming from the Gotthard and the Bernardine Passes

Die Wallfahrtskirche
Madonna del Sasso bei Locarno

L'église Madonna del Sasso, au-dessus
de Locarno, est un lieu de pèlerinage

The Pilgrim's Church of Madonna
del Sasso near Locarno

Ascona, malerischer Badeort
am Lago Maggiore

Ascona, une plage pittoresque
du lac Majeur

Ascona, a picturesque bathing-place
on Lake Maggiore

Brissago am Lago Maggiore

Brissago, au bord du lac Majeur

Brissago on Lake Maggiore

230   Blick vom Monte San Salvatore auf Lugano   Vue sur Lugano et le lac   Lugano, seen from San Salvatore

Autobahn bei Lugano. Im Hintergrund der Villenort Castagnola und
der Luganer See

L'autoroute près de Lugano.
A l'arrière-plan, les villas de
Castagnola et le lac de Lugano

Motorway near Lugano. In the background the wealthy residential district
of Castagnola and Lake Lugano

231

Alte Brücke über die Verzasca
bei Lavertezzo

Un vieux pont sur la Verzasca
près de Lavertezzo

Ancient bridge over the Verzasca
near Lavertezzo

Morcote, vielbesuchtes altertüm-
liches Städtchen am Luganer See

Morcote, petite ville très ancienne située sur le
lac de Lugano, est très recherchée des touristes

Morcote, a much-visited quaint
old town on Lake Lugano

233

Ponte Tresa, Grenzdorf am Ausfluß der Tresa aus dem Luganer
See

Ponte Tresa, village-frontière situé
à l'endroit où la Tresa sort du lac
de Lugano

Ponte Tresa, a border town situated at
the point where the River Tresa flows
out of Lake Lugano

Maggia-Delta und Lago Maggiore
im Tessin

Maggia-Delta et le Lac Majeur,
dans le Tessin

The delta of the River Maggia
and Lake Maggiore in Ticino

235

Printed in Germany